What This Book Will Do for You

If you want to get control, right now, over your life, this book will tell you how. By learning how to organize your life effectively and set firm goals, you will be able to put yourself on the road to career advancement and personal enrichment. So read on . . .

How to Control Your Life Through Self-Management

Get Organized!

Donald H. Weiss

amacom
American Management Association

This book is available at a special
discount when ordered in bulk quantities.
For information, contact Special Sales Department,
AMACOM, a division of American Management
Association, 135 West 50th Street, New York, NY 10020.

Library of Congress Cataloging-in-Publication Data

Weiss, Donald H., 1936-
    Get organized!

(The Successful office skills series)
    Includes index.
    1. Executives—Time management. I. Title. II. Series.
HD38.W4242   1986   658.4'093   85-26733
ISBN 0-8144-7646-5

Printing Number

10

CONTENTS

Introduction—Getting Control over Your Life

"If only I had more time in the day." Who among us has never shouted out to heaven that plaintive lament?

Or this equally sad refrain: "I'll never get all this done. I just don't have enough time."

Time. In the grand scheme of things, each one of us has but an hour in which to strut and fret, as Shakespeare said, and for many of us, it seems, we accomplish nothing. We make a great deal of noise while going about it—sound and fury, in the Bard's words—but in the end, we come away with very little of what we really wanted to accomplish.

Each day seems more hectic than the last. Each hour seems too cluttered with things to do for us to finish anything at all. The whole world comes crashing in on us just when we need to finish that report or get out that correspondence or meet with the boss about yet another project.

For those reasons I have to take issue with the great master of ideas when he says our tomorrows creep in a petty pace from day to day. Not so. The older we get, the faster our days fly away into yesterday, and our greatest fear is that we will never accomplish all that we've set out to do.

And why will so many of us leave undone all that we could've accomplished? Because we don't know how to get control over our lives. We let life control us.

Such was the case with Alice Brown, whose story I'll share with you shortly. She had no plan of her own—but all she needed to get control was to set some goals for herself, recognize which among them were most important to her, identify the objectives whereby she could achieve those goals, and design an action plan to follow.

That is what this book is all about. Getting control over your life. Over the big things and the small. Over the long term and the short. Over the whole of your life and over today, this minute, now.

Get control over your life, and you'll get control over your time.

Chapter 1

Self-Management— The How of Getting Control

Alice Brown, supervisor of bookkeeping in the finance and accounting department of Jones' Distribution and Supply, worked hard. No two ways about it. You could tell how hard she worked because her desk was always covered with papers, ledgers, books, and reports. She was *surrounded* by stacks of papers, ledgers, books, and reports.

She had all those stacks of papers organized, all right. "This stack on the left is stuff that has to get out right away. That stack on the right can wait awhile, and this stack in the middle is stuff that had to get out right away—yesterday. See. I know what I have to do, but it'll take an army of bookkeepers to get it all done."

She also worked long hours. Came in early some mornings, stayed late most evenings. Even missed lunch hours and coffee breaks.

But not so Alice's boss, Francine Miller, manager of finance and accounting. Now, I'm not saying that Francine didn't work as hard as Alice did. A self-made woman who had attended night school to become a CPA, while raising two children in the process, Francine was a self-confessed perfectionist. Every decimal point had its proper place; every deadline had the sanctity of holy sacrament. "I exercise self-management; I organize and control myself. I expect self-management from the people who work for me as well." No, Francine drove herself hard, but the way she did it made it look easy to everyone else—especially to Alice.

To hear Alice tell it, Francine looked so good to everyone else because, when it came to the real work, the manager just dumped everything on her. Alice insisted that she lived the life of a Cinderella, a charwoman on whom all projects were stacked without any consideration for when or how she could get them done.

Neither woman really cared all that much for the other. Francine tolerated Alice's bad work habits—habits that no amount of coaching had been able to eradicate—and Alice jealously abided Francine's perfectionism. And both women waited impatiently for the end of the year, when Frank Jones, the chief financial officer, would retire. Francine had been tapped to succeed him in that role.

Though no one had said anything yet, Alice was sure she'd get Francine's job. Well, let's put it this way, she *hoped* she'd get it. She'd heard rumors, however, that Bob Jones, the company's president, was considering bringing in someone else—perhaps a relative.

Alice had trouble believing the rumor. After all, she was the supervisor of bookkeeping, had been for three years—ever since Mr. Welsh died suddenly, leaving no one else to fill the slot. She had seniority in the company; she had all the technical skills for the job. But somehow or other, her life always seemed rushed, hurried, and harried. There was never enough time in the day to oversee or finish everything.

Alice never doubted that Francine caused all her troubles. Alice tried to live up to Francine's standards, but no matter how hard she tried, she made errors or let some of her clerks' errors slip by her. Oh, no big errors. Nothing resembling the disasters Francine always seemed to shout about. Well, maybe she didn't shout, but to Alice's ears, every complaint seemed to be shouted.

What was the big deal about someone's posting a bill incorrectly once in a while? So, sometimes they didn't get reports finished on time. Like the time Francine had demanded that Alice get the quarterly expense report finished and on her desk by no later than 9:00 on the first of October. It's true, she got it to the boardroom at 10:30, a half hour after the meeting started, but they hadn't reached that part of the agenda yet, had they?

"If you wouldn't just pile all the work on me," Alice countered, "maybe I could get it out on time."

Well, soon Francine would no longer be directly in charge of their department. "Ms. Efficiency," Alice harumphed when she heard that Francine would get the CFO position. "Little does anyone know that I make her look good. If I had as little to do as she, and if I prissed around the way she does, buttering up everyone, I'd get my promotion, too."

But Alice's promotion was not to be. Bob Jones brought in that "someone" from the outside—and not a relative—to manage the department.

To Alice, this is the way it always is. The quiet,

hardworking people—people who work late, arrive early, have piles of work on their desks all the time; people who have too much to do and not enough time in which to get it all done—what do they get? They review the ledgers, write up the financials, prepare the projections, oversee the billings, make the deposits—even make the coffee and serve it all around when Francine chairs a meeting. A smile and a grudging thank you, that's what they get.

"Sure we make mistakes, miss a few deadlines. We're only human. Is that reason enough to pass us by?"

Working Smarter
Through Goal-Directed Knowledge

How many "Alices"—men as well as women—do you know? People work themselves half to death, getting nowhere in a hurry, not knowing how to capitalize on an opportunity. For every Francine there must be literally hundreds of Alices. Their problem is not a matter of motivation. Lord knows, they want to get to the top. They wouldn't work so hard if they didn't want success. No, it's not a matter of desire; it's a question of *how to get control over their lives*—a question of what Francine called "self-management."

If poor Alice's sad story has a moral, it's this: *To get all that you want from your life, you have to work hard, but working smart makes working hard easier.* Wrap your eyes around those words a few times, and they'll make sense to you.

For most of us, working is the normal condition of survival. And most of us prefer demanding, challenging jobs to mundane, routine, repetitive tasks. So we take on complex jobs, look for ways to be creative, put out a lot of energy at getting the job done well, getting it done right. In short, we work hard.

Yet Alice makes her work harder for herself than it has to be. She lacks self-management skills. What chance *did* Alice have of filling the bill as manager of such an important staff function?

Maybe more of a chance than you think, if—the big "if".

The big "if" refers to Alice's taking a new approach, not just to her daily workload, but to her very life-style. Sloppiness, carelessness, and disorganization at work reflect a fundamental sense of floating through life, catching what you can along the way, usually by accident or in spite of yourself. To get her act together at work, Alice should have had her act together, period.

That's what *self-management* is all about. *It means getting control through goal-directed knowledge.* The whole thing starts with that word *goal.* It starts with your deciding what you want for yourself—not just immediately, but for your life as a whole. What kind of payoffs do you want from your work? Once you know what goals you'd like to achieve, then you can plan the objectives you need to reach and organize the activities you'll have to do to get there.

Self-Management versus Time Management—A Crucial Distinction

One significant issue that requires clarification here is how time management relates to self-management. The two concepts are *not* synonymous, even though time is an important factor in self-management. And what most people call time management means very little without what I call self-management.

Time management is clock-oriented. You focus your

attention on time itself. Most time-management systems reinforce that concentration on the clock by requiring you to keep "time logs" and do "time-log analyses." You spend your whole day, your whole week, your whole month referring to clocks and calendars.

Time management considered this way creates an unnecessary and self-defeating time pressure. Time pressure then creates stress, which interferes with effectiveness. And poor Alice, she's not even efficient, let alone effective.

She knows what her job is, and she knows how to do everything her job requires. But to be effective, she has to learn how to *achieve her specified goals and/or objectives by a given deadline and in order of priority.* And that requires self-management.

The focus of self-management is on the *goal,* on what has to be accomplished or achieved or reached. In my approach, I treat time as just one more goal, a target to be reached—a measure of success.

I'll now backtrack in this story about Alice to illustrate my point. Remember how she was supposed to get the quarterly expense report to Francine by 9:00 on October 1? Remember, also, that she didn't get it to the meeting until 10:30? It's true, they hadn't reached that part of the agenda yet, but still, by not being on time, Alice hadn't done her job effectively, and Francine couldn't do hers effectively either.

Oh, Alice's time was managed, all right—but only in the sense that her time was *planned.* She was *supposed* to get the job done by 9:00. But her *life* wasn't managed, and *she missed her deadline.*

Another way of saying that is that Alice had an objective, an intermediate goal with respect to the company's meeting. Her primary question, the one she probably never asked, is, *"What do I have to do to accomplish that goal?"*

Deciding What You Want

The question of what you must do to accomplish your goals illustrates the fundamental approach to life to which I referred earlier. Self-management begins with deciding what you want out of life in general and work in particular. To make those decisions, you must answer two sets of crucial questions. The first set will help you to identify your routine or repetitive tasks. These responsibilities you can schedule in advance, leaving you time to develop unusual or creative goals in your work and in your life. These questions are:

1. What do I have to do every day?
2. What do I have to do periodically?
3. What do I have to do infrequently?

The second set of questions listed here will aid you in setting priorities and planning for contingencies:

1. Of all the things I have to do, which ones contribute the most toward achieving my goals?
2. What are the most *immediate* things to be done, and why should I do them first?
3. What are things that get in the way of my achieving my goals, and why do they happen?
4. What can I do to prevent problems from becoming crises (how can I become proactive rather than reactive)?

You manage what you do, not time, in order to accomplish your goals and/or objectives. And that's a most important part of *the definition of management: achieving goals through the proper utilization of resources.* The main resource you have for getting control over your own life is yourself. Therefore, pay less attention to the clock and more attention to yourself. *Instead of futilely trying to manage time, manage yourself.*

Chapter 2

*Goals and Objectives—
The Road Map to Control*

Not until Francine's promotion had been announced did Alice really consider becoming manager of finance and accounting. Could it have been that she didn't make it because she didn't start out on that journey through the company when she first came to work there?

In the beginning Alice had only a vague idea that she'd like to get somewhere in life. She fell into her supervisory job, and only when the management job opened up did the idea of filling it attract her. She had no clearly recognizable or well-formulated goals, and without those goals for her life and career, she had become disoriented, lost. She had no destination in mind or any idea of how to get there. The clutter on her desk merely mirrored the clutter of her whole life.

I'll make this perfectly clear by an analogy. You've taken road trips before, and you probably know something about reading a road map. If we lived in a one-dimensional world, the journey from start to finish might look like the straightforward process shown in the accompanying diagram. But how many journeys are quite that simple? And obviously, no one's life or career is that simple either. You need an itinerary, a plan.

Hired⸺⸺▶ Supervisor ⸺⸺▶ Manager

Whether you're talking about your life, your career, or your job (or some part of it), the plan is the first step toward success. That success, however, depends on the thoroughness with which you do your planning. Alice knew that the expense report had to be on Francine's desk by October 1 at 9:00, but she saw only a statement of a target to be reached. The steps required for achieving that goal—those were the ingredients missing from the plan.

The Goal—What You Want to Accomplish

Stop for a moment and look at a road map of the United States, tracing a route from New York to Miami. It becomes quite readily apparent that the route you choose is only one of many. Yet certain features about setting up an itinerary—any itinerary—always remain the same.

This holds true for career planning, for overall job planning, and for daily planning alike. The place toward which you're heading—let's say, manager of finance and accounting—that's the goal, the destination, the end point of the trip. When you reach that point, the journey itself has come to an end. You now set about to achieve other goals—to build the department, to return to school to earn a CPA, and so on. You reach for new heights, seek new ways to stretch yourself and move out of your comfort zone.

That's what I mean by a *goal*—it's an end point, a final destination. Whether it's in the distant or immediate future, it's what you want to accomplish or achieve, and when you achieve a particular goal, all activity related to achieving that goal stops. Without a goal, you have no idea of where you want to go. With a goal, you not only get where you want to go, but you can then set about to achieve further goals.

Objectives—Milestones Along the Road to Your Goal

But beyond an overriding goal, if you're going to get the most out of your life or career, you've got more planning to do than Alice has done—and that's where objectives come in.

Even if Alice had set out from the beginning to become the manager of finance and accounting, she hadn't planned her course thoroughly. She met only some of the objectives she would have had to achieve in order to have reached her goal. She learned her bookkeeping and accounting skills, but she never learned how to apply them effectively. That's the same as planning a trip by saying only, "We'll get in our car, we'll start our trip in New York, and somehow, eventually, we'll get to Miami." That approach leaves out some pretty important intermediate steps.

How do I become more efficient, more organized? How do I become an effective supervisor—not only liked by my employees and boss, but also respected by them. What other steps do I have to take to become a manager? Each question involves a planned stop along the path toward a career goal. Each stop is called a milestone, one more step toward reaching the final goal—management.

That's what an objective is—a milestone in a plan for accomplishing a goal. Whereas the goal stands by itself and may have no reason for being other than, "That's what I want, 'cause I want it," an objective, or milestone, exists only because it leads to something else. Even if you enjoy being a supervisor, if you really want to be a manager, you're in your present position only because you had to reach that milestone in your journey to the top. A milestone is a measure of accomplishment. It tells you where you are with respect to your final destination. In fact, only by counting milestones can you tell whether or not you will ever reach your goal. Since deadlines are also objectives, time enters into your planning as an objective—to achieve an intermediate destination or your final destination *by a predetermined time.*

Objectives differ from goals in still another way. A goal stands on its own. Once you achieve it, all activity toward accomplishing it ceases. This is not necessarily so with an objective. Even though you've reached a milestone (achieved an objective), other milestones still exist before you can reach your final destination. You now have to set out to reach the other milestones.

Many people don't realize what they're getting into when they take a long road trip, or enter into a new career, or take on a new job because they haven't planned all the milestones thoroughly or taken a good look at what lies ahead. That's what I said of Alice just a little while ago.

Chapter 3

Planning—Giving Your Life Your Best Shot

There are no guarantees in life, but really serious planning is a sincere attempt to know what you have to do to get to where you want to go and what pitfalls you may have to overcome to get there.

It's your life. Isn't it worth the effort?

I'll stop here and let you take a look at the accompanying sidebar, in which I offer some concise definitions for the words I've been using to talk about planning—*goal* and *objective*—and introduce you to another term: *goal statement.* Then, I'll use those words to show you how Alice could have designed an actual plan for becoming the manager of finance and accounting.

Some Key Words

Goal: An end point—that which you want to accomplish as a final result or end product of your efforts. A payoff from and for your efforts.

Objective: A step toward accomplishing a goal, a milestone, an intermediate goal; a measure of your success in accomplishing the ultimate goal of your effort.

Goal Statement: The expression of a desired result, whether it be an ultimate goal or an objective; it consists of a target, a deadline, and the means or conditions that affect achieving the result.

Defining Your Target—
The Goal Statement

If Alice had known about the little device called "a goal statement," her life would have been entirely different, because a well-formulated goal statement is the backbone of any plan. Yet most people founder right here—confusing the target of a goal statement with the plan as a whole. So let's spend a moment considering goal statements.

Many managers get themselves in trouble when they say, "All I want to know about is *the bottom line.*" Well, the bottom line may tell the profit-or-loss story, but that's the last page of the book. If you read only the solution to the mystery, you miss the best parts. Even the most profitable companies can, like a mystery novel, fall apart internally if the "how did we get here?" is ignored.

No, the success of any effort depends upon a critical evaluation of the conditions and contingencies that will affect how well you'll achieve your target within the time frame you've set for yourself. That means looking at the whole plan, a plan based on a measurable, or at least observable, realistic target—one that, with the information available to you, you believe you can achieve.

Consider a few more important words: *measurable, observable, realistic, achievable.* If it's possible to assign a number to your target—to quantify it, as in "earn $35,000 a year"—do it. If numbers aren't applicable, use words that describe something you can feel, hear, smell, taste, or see—as in, "become the manager of finance and accounting." That's what I mean by measurable or observable.

When you describe your target in one of those ways (or in some combination of the two), it's much easier to decide if it's realistic or achievable. If you're untrained or undereducated and earning $15,000 a year now, applying today for a technical job paying $35,000 may prove as futile as Alice's hoping to land Francine's job without making some significant changes in her life.

Chapter 4

Goals and the Seven Dimensions of a Whole Person

The only way to keep your day and your desktop free from irrelevant or unnecessary mishmash is to keep your life free from irrelevant or unnecessary clutter. *You do that by knowing what you're doing at all times—and why you're doing it. That means knowing not only what your goals are but also how they fit together.*

Tangible and Intangible Goals

The way I've described the targets of goals so far includes only one type of goal: tangible goals. The other type of goal is called intangible goals.

Goals can also be divided to reflect the seven dimensions of a person's life: career, financial, family relations, material goods, social relations, community relations, and personal values. Only by looking at goals this way can you integrate the different aspects of your life—bridging the gap between working for a living and living.

Tangible payoffs are those you can touch, see, feel, hear, smell. Listed under this heading are income, things of monetary value, and other aspects of your physical life—even if you collect material things as a way of getting some type of nonmaterial personal satisfaction, such as finding pleasure in looking at beautiful artwork or taking pride in ownership.

However, intangible payoffs don't usually come together in the same package with material things. Instead, people usually tie their intangible goals to spiritual or intellectual values; to emotional states, such as love; or to feelings, such as happiness. Family relations, social and community relations, religious values, and other such bits and pieces of life fall under this heading.

Stop and think about it for a moment. Which of your goals—which of the payoffs you want from what you do—are most important to you? Tangible or intangible? Can you get the payoffs you want from your present kind of work or at the place where you now work? If not, what will you have to do to get them? In order to answer that question, you first have to decide in what dimension of your life that payoff lies.

The Wholistic Approach to Goal Setting

Little happens in a person's life that falls outside one or more of the dimensions that are briefly described in the sidebar on page 18. In order to get more control over your life, you have to take better notice of everything that happens to you, and planning consists of arranging those dimensions to take into account your most important values and payoffs. Planning gives you a basis for concentrating your attention on one or more of those dimensions at any given moment.

Paying attention to the dimensions of your life makes you more than efficient. It makes you *effective.*

Efficient people do their jobs well. They do whatever they do the right way. Effective people do whatever they do the right way, too, but more than that, *they do the right job, at the right time, in the right place.* They look at the goals they want to achieve, at the dimensions of their lives in which those goals lie, and they do what is necessary in those areas to reach their goals. They mix the objectives of two or more dimensions only when doing so furthers the achievement of a goal or goals.

Study the sidebar on page 18 before coming back to this text. Once you digest that material, you'll have a secure base for making the decisions that self-management requires.

In which dimension do you find your most important goals? Into what do you put most of your energy every day? Do you ever find yourself mixing the goals of two or more dimensions in such a way that they interfere with each other? How can you stop that? How can you combine dimensions in order to maximize your ability to achieve your goals in all the dimensions?

Using the career plan Alice should have designed years ago, I'll illustrate only three of those seven dimensions: income, career, and family relations. I'll also have to add to your knowledge about Alice in order for you to see how the connections between the dimensions are made.

Alice is now a single parent, but even when she was married, she wanted to be self-sufficient, a high-income earner, and a good provider for her two young children. She wants to raise her children in a suburban,

Seven Dimensions of a Whole Person

Financial

Levels of income; the amount of money you would like to earn at different stages of your life and over the course of your lifetime.

Career

The types of activities in which you want to engage in order to earn your income and the status in your profession that you would like to achieve.

Family

The kinds of relationships you want to have with your relatives (for example, your immediate family, your spouse).

Material Goods

The types of things you want to own (such as a house, automobiles, furniture, clothing).

Social Relations

The kinds of relationships you wish to have with people other than your family (such as with friends and acquaintances).

Community Relations

The status you wish to achieve where you live (for instance, an elected official or a volunteer leader in church or synagogue).

Personal Values

The quality of health that you wish to maintain, the degree of literacy and awareness that you want to reach, the spiritual values that are important to you.

ranch-style house. She also wants to have fun times with them—vacations and the like.

You can see that some aspects of her family relations—such as the desire to raise her children in a suburban, ranch-style house—depend entirely on income (which also overlaps the dimension of material things). That income, in turn, depends on career. Other aspects of that dimension—for instance, love and affection—don't depend on income or career but can be affected by either or both. In short, family relations, income, and career, although separate dimensions, touch on each other at a variety of points.

Income depends on career, but only in part. Career affects family relations and vice versa, but only at times. A goal in one dimension ("have an income of $50,000 a year") becomes an objective in another dimension ("buy a suburban, ranch-style house").

Keeping the dimensions separate when appropriate helps you keep yourself on track toward one goal at a time. For example, when at work, you're working on either a financial goal or a career goal. Letting family-relations goals interfere with work-related activities could become an obstacle to reaching the financial or career goal.

Taking a wholistic approach to goal setting allows you to separate pathways along which to plan your daily activities—a career path, a financial path, and so on—or combine them when appropriate.

So now, you'll be taking a look at the anatomy of a goal statement, and as you do so, remember to apply your effort to what Alice could have done but didn't. Yet don't do what so many other people do. Don't make all kinds of plans in your mind and, before getting a chance to implement your plans, forget them. That's a surefire way for paving the road to hell with good intentions.

The best-laid plans are written (with paper and pencil, not in concrete). At least this way, you have a guide for your journey, even if at one time or another you take an eraser to some part of the plan.

Chapter 5

How an Achievable Goal Statement Leads to Success

The future Alice wanted for herself didn't happen. Once she finally decided on her target, she had no plan for hitting it.

As I've said, a plan is like a map, insofar as it's a chart to follow once you make up your mind to follow it. It's a chart with a destination, with alternative routes, and in a sense, a built-in mileage chart (the deadlines). It even outlines how to mobilize your resources for making your journey more comfortable and identifies the obstacles that might get in the way of your reaching the target.

As I show you how to develop your own plan, I'll be spelling out Alice's plan on forms identical to the blank ones you'll find at the end of the book. As I talk about the plan she never wrote, work along on a plan of your own, completing each step in turn.

A wise philosopher once said, "A journey of a thousand miles begins with but one step."

The First Step—
Setting Realistic, but Challenging, Goals

If you're going to get control over your daily life, the first step in that long journey has to consist of setting realistic, achievable goals that you can fulfill in a reasonable period of time. Whether you're setting tangible or intangible goals, and regardless of the dimension they pertain to, they must be realistic. At the same time, they should challenge you as well. If you take on far more than you can actually accomplish, you'll create a sense of panic that will stop you from doing anything at all. But if you don't try to stretch yourself, you'll just work as hard as ever going nowhere.

Thinking that you can do anything you set your mind to do is an essential ingredient to success. Knowing your own limitations, however, is just as important—as long as you don't use your awareness as an excuse for not trying. Realistic, achievable goals take into account both your ambitions and your boundaries.

A goal statement consists of a target, a deadline, and a set of means or conditions by which the goal will be accomplished. The target, when referring to the final goal, is called the end point; when referring to an objective, it's called a milestone. The deadline indicates by when you want to reach your target—whether the target is a goal or an objective. *And each element of the goal statement must be tested for its achievability and realism.*

The descriptions in the sidebar on page 22 will help you measure the achievability and realism of your own goals. Take a look at them before continuing with your reading.

What Makes a Goal Achievable

For a goal to be achievable

- Your decisions must be *deliberately* and *consciously* made—must *come from yourself,* be imposed *by you on yourself,* and be based on *your own* values, wishes, desires, or needs.
- It must be part of *a system* of goals and objectives that reflects your values, wishes, desires, and needs and that *covers every dimension of life important to you.*
- It must *reflect payoffs* you honestly believe are *within your reach* rather than a fantasy, be *challenging* while taking into account your own *real limitations.*
- It must be *specific* rather than vague and general, with a *target,* a *deadline,* and the *conditions under which they both can be reached.*

An achievable goal

- Is based on *serious reflection* on your values and your expectations of yourself and can be used for *making decisions* as to what to do *right now* as well as later on.
- Forms the *standards* and the *criteria* by which you judge the value of the alternative courses available to you as well as your degree of success.
- Focuses your attention on the *consequences* of your actions and helps you identify the *priorities.*
- Helps build *self-confidence.*
- *Saves time and energy* by creating *order and purpose;* becomes your *motivation;* becomes what you *want* to achieve.

Now, let's take Alice's goal—to become the manager of finance and accounting. That's the target. It's realistic, insofar as she has the bookkeeping and accounting education as well as supervisory experience. It's achievable because her decision is deliberately and consciously made, based on her own values, wishes, desires, and needs. It can now be made a part of a system of goals and objectives, and definite standards or criteria for success can be developed.

A Practical Tool—
The Worksheet for Creating
a Well-Formulated Goal Statement

The work of designing Alice's plan can be done on the format on page 24, called a Worksheet for Creating a Well-Formulated Goal Statement. This one instrument, by focusing on *goals and objectives,* makes it possible to create a plan that will enable you to get control over everyday life by getting control over your future.

When completed, the goal statement will help you sort out who will do what, when, why, where, and how. The goal statement will give you the basis from which you can design an action plan.

The end result of this part of Alice's planning, then, will be a statement that reads:

When Francine is promoted or leaves the company, become the manager of finance and accounting by learning all I can about bookkeeping, accounting, and financial planning; by learning how to organize my own work; by learning how to distribute and delegate work; by learning how to oversee the work of other people, coaching and counseling them rather than

Worksheet for Creating a Well-Formulated Goal Statement

Target: Become the manager of finance & accounting

Deadline: When Francine is promoted or leaves the company

Conditions

Milestones: By learning all I can about bookkeeping, accounting, and financial planning

By learning how to organize my own work

By learning how to distribute and delegate work

By learning how to oversee the work of other people, coaching and counseling them rather than doing their work for them when they make errors

Contingencies: Falling into sloppy work habits

Letting problems at home interfere with my concentration at work

Not having enough money to pay for my tuition

doing their work for them when they make errors. I'll also be careful to avoid falling into sloppy work habits, to avoid letting problems at home interfere with my concentration at work, and to earmark a portion of my budget for personal education.

Read over the accompanying worksheet from which this well-formulated goal statement was put together. Then, pick out one of your own personal targets. You're going to produce some worksheets for yourself covering at least *three goals* you want to pursue.

As you work on your own plan, when listing the milestones, list all the things you can think of that you might have to accomplish, both to prepare for and to reach your target. Be thorough. List whatever comes into your head. You may want to make some changes in those milestones later, but that's O.K. That's why you use pencil and paper instead of chisel and stone.

When you get through with that list, start on the contingencies. Those are all the things you can think of that can possibly prevent you from reaching your target. To complete your action planning, you'll turn your contingencies into a game of "What if." This way, you'll be in control of your life's crises, instead of letting your life's crises control you.

Stay relatively general. No detail. Save the detail for the action planning. When developing a goal statement, you want to keep it focused on goals and objectives, not on specific things to do to reach your targets. The goal statement helps you sort out who does what, when, why, where, and how; that is, the goal statement gives you the basis from which you can later design the action plan.

Once you've completed this task, return to your reading here.

Chapter 6

Converting Goals into Actions

Now you've got your well-formulated goal statement. But you're far from finished.

That's right. After all that work, you still don't have *the plan.* You know where you're heading; you know what milestones you have to reach to get there; and you have some idea of the problems you could encounter along the way. Nonetheless, even if it's not *the plan,* it's one heck of a lot more than Alice had to start with. Converting goals into actions requires three crucial steps: (1) setting priorities; (2) answering the questions of who, what, why, where, when, and how; and (3) playing "What if."

Setting Priorities Among Goals

When you listed your milestones, if you're like most people, you probably tried to list things *chronologically*—in a logical *sequence* of steps.

That's good. That's one part of setting priorities. Other considerations concern questions of *immediacy* and *importance.*

Goals, especially important ones, often compete among themselves for fulfillment (taking a trip to Miami versus buying a house or finishing a project at work). Goals, as distinguished from objectives, compete with each other in terms of their importance to you or to someone close to you—a loved one, a boss. No matter how important a goal is to someone else, however, it comes down to how badly *you* want to accomplish it—the urgency *you* feel. In short, you value a goal in terms of its importance and/or immediacy to *you*.

If, in this make-believe plan for Alice, she were dealing with realities, she'd have to ask, Which is more important to me right now? Having my evenings free to spend with the children or going to school at night to become a CPA? Is becoming the manager of finance and accounting the only way to earn enough money to buy the suburban ranch-style house, or should I pursue some other goal?

A goal is important only because you want to fulfill it. Deciding on whether or not you want something to happen involves emotional issues and often depends on value judgments that you have made or that someone else has made ("That's good") or on a desire ("I want it") or on a need ("It makes me happy").

Decisions like those depend on gut-level experiences and/or feelings more often than on objective criteria. You frequently make the decision in favor of one goal rather than another by answering the question, Just how badly do I want one rather than, or before, the other?

At the same time, deciding just how important a goal is to you needn't be a totally irrational process. You can sort it all out a little more rationally by asking yourself the following short list of questions and answering them honestly:

1. What would happen if I *don't* accomplish this goal?
2. If I don't, who would be affected and how?
3. If I don't, will the end results be positive or negative with respect to my other goals as well as those of the family, the company, the department, my other associations, and so on?

4. If nothing bad or of consequence happens if I *don't* accomplish the goal, why work for it?
5. If something good would happen if I *do* achieve it, then why not put everything necessary into doing it and doing it right?

As you can see, even those questions are loaded with value words: *bad, good.* The imply "should" or "ought" or "should not" or "ought not." But at least the questions force you to state reasons for the values.

You may want to stop at this point and take pencil and paper to the targets of your three well-formulated goal statements. Make some preliminary decisions as to which is the most important goal for you to pursue at this time. Then continue reading in the following section on how to evaluate the priorities among milestones.

Setting Priorities Among Milestones

In some ways it's easier to set priorities for milestones. And for the same reason, in some ways, it's harder.

Priorities for milestones come from much more objective criteria than do priorities for goals. So on the one hand, you can minimize the gut-level stuff that often causes confusion and sometimes conflict between your goals and other people; on the other hand, you must become much more conscious of accuracy, precision, and honesty when setting priorities among objectives. Becoming conscious of those things isn't always as easy as it seems.

Of the two issues—immediacy and dependency—with which you have to deal, immediacy is the less complicated matter, and it gives me a chance to talk about time: the deadlines you set for accomplishing goals or reaching milestones.

Academically speaking, a deadline is a standard or a

measure by which you judge or evaluate your effectiveness in reaching some point in space or on a time-measuring instrument—a clock or a calendar. More simply stated, a deadline is the time a goal or an objective should be reached. Time is a measure of success. Its importance rests in when the job gets done, the house is purchased, or you reach your milestones or destination. In this respect, talking about when to *stop* a project or journey or when to achieve a goal is the easy part of the criterion of immediacy.

The hard part is deciding on when the process should *start*. Though it doesn't seem like it, most people allow themselves more time than they need to get a job done. Then they say, "Well, I've got loads of time," and they put off to another day what they should have started today. Then, suddenly, they come back to reality with a start. "Oh, my God. Where'd the time go? I never have enough time to get all this work done." (Are you reading this, Alice?)

Other people try to cram too much into too short a time period. They just don't stop to think about how much work or effort has to go into any one project or into any one part of a project when they set about to reach their goals. They plan unrealistically.

Still a third group of people simply procrastinate. They know what they have to do and how much time they have for doing it. They often set realistic time goals. Then, for some reason, they stop; even the best-laid plans do nothing to help them.

Only deciding on the reason(s) for procrastinating and making a conscious effort to deal with the situation will help you alter the way things are. Sometimes the situation demands an honest (See? There's one of those tough words) self-appraisal as well as a frank talk with your boss, your spouse, or a counselor before it can be resolved.

But now, let's get more to the point. When planning, how do you decide on the immediacy with which you have to attack something, especially an objective that would lead to achieving a goal?

First, do a little exercise that illustrates what I mean when I say that people really don't know how to gauge time well. In the accompanying sidebar (Reading Exercise 1), you'll find several paragraphs (taken from another book I wrote) that I want you to read. Before you start reading them, take off your watch, and turn away from your clock(s). Now, check the time before you start to read, and complete as much of the material as you can in what you *think* is the elapsed time of *two minutes.* If you finish the reading before you think the two minutes are up, start again and continue reading until the time elapses.

When you think two minutes have elapsed, stop and check the time. Do *not* check the time *before* you stop. Stop *when you think the time is up,* then check the time.

Now read the exercise. Move on to the material that follows only after you have completed it.

Reading Exercise 1

Men concerned with practical, social, or economic pursuits can't afford to question their own beliefs, to examine the formulae by which they put their practices into operation. Businessmen, scientists, and revolutionaries are alike in that if they ever stopped to question the truth of the principles they employ to make their operations meaningful, they would probably face Hamletlike dilemmas.

And philosophy, too, usually follows on the heels of deeds. It is *ex post facto.* It systematically expresses and examines beliefs of a moment passing out of existence, yet leaving their imprint on succeeding moments. Rarely does the philosopher himself create a revolution; rather, he systematically formulates the beliefs and attitudes of his generation.

Often, sometimes by mere chance, he affects the lives of generations that follow—but merely by giving direction to a revolution already in progress. The writings of Harrington, Locke, and Voltaire express the mercantile liberalism of the newly emerging middle class, and when read by Jefferson, Madison, and Adams, find their way into the political and social institutions of the new American nation. The writings of Karl Marx express the social and economic aspirations of the working class, and when read by Lenin, Mao, and Castro, shape the destinies of millions of people (and still operate vigorously as a doctrine of revolution). The writings of Nietzsche, Kierkegaard, and Dostoevski express the fears and concerns of nineteenth-century people faced with the mechanization of their lives, and when read by Sartre, Camus, and Gide, give voice to the anxieties of people faced with the computerization of their lives.

Adapted from Weiss, Donald H. *Why Study Philosophy?* Fort Worth, Tex.: American Continental Publishing Company, 1970.

- -

How much time elapsed before you stopped? Write the elapsed time on a sheet of paper.

Most people fall short of the two minutes, some by as much as a whole minute. Some go over the two minutes by as much as 30 to 45 seconds. Very few people ever hit two minutes on the dot. That's because our awareness of time depends on clocks, not on some inner sense.

But more important, how many lines of material did you read? Write that number, too, on the sheet of paper.

Surprised? If you're like most people, you probably finished fewer lines than you thought you would. After all, there are only three paragraphs of text.

Yet what were you really thinking about when you were doing that exercise? The subject matter or the time?

Most people think about the time, not about the reading. The time requirement creates time pressures, and few people think clearly about the two things at the same time. Those people who run over the two minutes finish more reading, not only because they use more time but also because they use more time as a consequence of concentrating on the reading rather than on the time.

O.K. Do the same exercise, this time with the material in the second accompanying sidebar (Reading Exercise 2), and this time *set a goal* for yourself as to the number of lines you want to read or think you should be able to read within the two minutes. Write that goal on your sheet of paper.

Follow the same instructions as you did in the first part of this exercise. Stop here and read the exercise before going any further.

Reading Exercise 2

Until recently, the important philosophic doctrines were European in origin, European in content, European in outlook. The American was still too busy, too oriented toward the economically practical to give his mind philosophic wings. Not until the late nineteenth century and during the early decades of the twentieth do scholars from the United States make significant contributions to the traditional discussions of metaphysics, epistemology, and ethics.

At the end of a century marked by civil war, religious revolution, the mechanization of agriculture, and an invasion of southern and eastern Europeans on the beachheads Anglo-Americans believed to be forever secured for themselves, four men brought prestige to American philosophic scholarship: Josiah Royce, a student of Hegel; Charles Sanders Peirce, influenced by the newly emerging mathematical physics and by the American experience itself; William James, a psychologist; and John Dewey, also a psychologist.

Significantly, this intellectual growth occurs during a short period (about 50 years) in the well-established centers in the eastern United States. There, heavily endowed institutions of higher-education and a relative ease of life provide the intellectual embryo with a placenta sufficiently rich in nourishment for rapid, healthy development. Fertilized by European scholarship, but carefully cultivated in the American womb, the new intellectuals—James and Dewey, in particular—did not attempt merely to perpetuate the old-world culture, but rather, heeding Ralph Waldo Emerson's advice to the American scholar, they attempted to develop a uniquely American overview.

Adapted from Weiss, Donald H. *Why Study Philosophy?* Fort Worth, Tex.: American Continental Publishing Company, 1970.

- -

All right. How much time elapsed before you stopped? How many lines did you read? Write both numbers on your sheet of paper.

Compare your times and numbers of lines completed. Did you run over this time or run over more than you did before? A few people still fall short, but most people *run over* or *run longer*—because their focus shifts. Their focus shifts from the two minutes to *the number of lines to read.* They shift their focus from a clock orientation to a *goal* orientation. The task, not the time, dominates their minds. The time pressure is reduced, and *they usually read more lines than they thought they could.*

I'll make the point painfully obvious. Setting realistic deadlines begins with your having a realistic sense of the relative importance of time itself. Compared to the goal to be achieved or the milestone to be reached, time loses its importance. The urgency of the target (its importance) dictates the time considerations—even if it means putting other activities or goals aside for now.

Then, evaluating the demands of the task(s) required for reaching the milestones dictates the deadlines for them. That requires recognizing the point of the exercise:

Allow yourself enough time to do what you have to do, but don't allow so long that you have too much time to spare.

Well, no one can tell you how long a job or a task well done should take until it's actually measured. In the workplace, there are many work-measurement systems that can help you and/or your supervisor set time standards for your job. For non–work-related activities, only you can be the best judge of when to start on the course toward some goal or how long it should take to get there.

On the other hand, I can share with you some guidelines to help you time-out any task, at work or at home. They'll help you set your starting and stopping points, and they'll also help you procrastinators get some control over that all-too-human tendency.

I've stated the guidelines in the accompanying sidebar as a list of questions for you to answer. Given any set of objectives, your answers to these questions should help you decide when to start and when to stop whatever it is you have to do.

- -

Six Ways of Measuring Immediacy

1. What has to be done in order to accomplish the objective(s)?
2. What has to be done first in order that other things can happen?
3. What part of the process is the most complicated or the most difficult, or about which part of the process do I know the least, and how long will it take to complete that aspect of the task?
4. Who needs this task completed, why is it important to him or her, and by when does he or she need it done or want it done?
5. What would happen if I miss the deadlines set? What would be the negative consequences, if any, for me or for others?
6. How important is it that I meet the demands of the task, especially if the deadlines are set by someone else?

- -

Two issues should make themselves apparent. First the goals of other people often create the immediacy of one of your own goals. "We need a decision today." "I need that new design for the marketing department by Wednesday." That decision or that design may have a low priority for you, but if the other person's position or authority carries significant weight, you may have to let his or her priority take precedence over yours. Not only are priorities relative to the people creating them, but the priorities themselves can create interpersonal conflicts between managers and employees, between spouses, between parents and children. It never hurts to check out the relative importance of goals with the people closest to you.

The second issue relates to question 2 in the sidebar—What has to be done first in order that other things can happen?

Remember, objectives are milestones on the journey to achieving a goal. Sometimes you have to achieve one or more objectives *in order to go on to reaching other objectives*. Since Alice wants to get her CPA, to be eligible to take her certification exams, she has to complete specific courses—first. The courses may be interesting and valuable in themselves, but with respect to the plan, their importance lies in their place in the chronology of things.

Immediacy is often determined not only by the degree of importance an objective or an activity has but also by the extent to which other things are dependent on it. That's why I single out this question and call it the

---

The Criterion of Dependency

1. For other things to happen, what do I have to accomplish or do first?
2. What depends on the achievement of this objective or on the doing of an activity?
3. What is the price of inaction?
4. If I do not achieve this objective or do this thing, what would happen or what would not happen that should? Can I do other things without doing this one?

---

criterion of dependency. In the accompanying sidebar, I spell out the questions you need to answer in order to apply this criterion as well as the criterion of importance and the criterion of immediacy.

Priorities—A Summation

Pulling all this information together requires separating your ideas into priorities for goals and priorities for objectives. Here's a rule of thumb for setting priorities for goals:

The highest-priority items are those that make the greatest demands and should have the highest rate of return for you from among all the goals in your personal list. Anything less than that should be relegated to second- or third-level priorities.

A rule of thumb for setting priorities among objectives is

An objective is imperative and has to be attacked first if it is not only important (in the sense described immediately above) but also carries with it a sense of urgency or immediacy, especially if its urgency is tied to the criterion of dependency.

When all is said and done, my whole point boils down to:

"You gotta wanna do it, and you gotta wanna do it now."

Self-Management—The "Want To"

Before you do a practice run in setting priorities, let's consider the "want to." I made an issue of procrastination earlier for a reason.

We usually put off those things we really don't want to do. We usually don't want to do those things because they don't fit with the goals we've set for ourselves. Counselors or psychotherapists see countless numbers of people whose "want to" has been reduced to "won't." And as with Alice, their work is stacked up all around them; they're backed up and behind schedule; they make too many errors, and they waste material and energy.

The popular notion of "burnout" is an exaggerated form of a "want to" turning into a "won't." For whatever reason, the motivation to continue doing what you once attacked with some degree of enthusiasm has flown away. Though people talk of burnout on the job more frequently than in other areas of life, parents can become as burned out with their roles as can nurses or teachers. Marriages, too, can suffer from burnout.

Burnout occurs when you decide that what you're doing really doesn't fit with what you want for yourself (though at one time you thought it did or would). Or you feel burnout when what you want for yourself changes, and what you're doing no longer fits with what you want now. The headaches, the fatigue, the dependence on drugs (including alcohol) that we associate with burnout are symptoms of frustration, a feeling that whatever it is you're doing just isn't worth the effort.

Creating a well-formulated goal statement and designing a thorough action plan for some dreaded project die aborning. A truly well-organized desk and calendar depend upon a truly well-organized life. For starters, a well-organized life depends on the integration of your work-related and life-related goals.

What you do at work becomes important to you only if those things fit with what you want to do with your life as a whole and in general. Organizing your work satisfactorily and effectively starts here, when you make those fundamental decisions concerning your own life.

Is this really what I want for myself? What would I feel if I were to quit doing what I'm doing? What would I do if I weren't doing this? In the direction I'm going and at the rate I'm getting there, when my life reaches its end, will I be able to lie back and say I have few, if any, regrets?

If you are among the fortunate few whose answers to those questions lead you to conclude confidently that you're heading in the right direction, then you feel a strong motivation to continue in your right path. Motivation of any kind, including the motivation to work or to work at a particular job, comes from within—from the needs, desires, or wishes that everyone has.

When those needs, desires, or wishes get very intense, they become our drivers—the discomforts that push us out of our comfort zones and into action. At any level of intensity, those needs, desires, or wishes lie behind all our goals. When what we do satisfies those needs, desires, or wishes, we'll do anything we can to make our effort most effective.

Think about it. No rewards your company or your supervisor or anyone else can give you can be as motivating as accomplishing your own goals. What are company rewards anyway? Your pay check. Bonuses. Promotions. Recognition. All are means to your own ends—means toward accomplishing your personal goals.

Therefore, if you're not meeting your personal goals through what you do to earn a living, or in the marriage in which you find yourself, or in the friendships you have, or in the leisure activities in which you engage, or with the things or properties you own, your first step toward self-management has to consist of finding new ways to meet your needs, desires, or wishes.

As radical as that idea may seem at first reading, it suggests a point you may not have considered for yourself. Namely, you may not know yet what needs, wishes, or desires you really want to meet. You may not have any personal goals, or you may not have any personal goals expressed as well-formulated goal statements. It could be that the reason you experience discomfort in the workplace, in your marriage or whatever, is that you haven't seen how those things fit together with what can be called your long-range personal goals. Only when you pull your personal goals together into a collection of well-formulated goal statements can you see if your current objectives match what you really want for yourself.

When you have a set of well-formulated personal goal statements, you can compare your organization's stated goals and your objectives within those goals to see if they do, in fact, relate to what you want for yourself. You can do the same with any set of relationships you have—from friends to marriage to leisure activities. If your personal goals and your goals within those relationships fit together, you'll find designing life and/or work plans relatively easy. If you then work the plan diligently, you'll find yourself at peace with yourself and with other people—and you'll find that your work will be easier, no matter how complex or energy-consuming that work happens to be.

On the other hand, if they don't fit together, designing your plan becomes even more important. Getting control over your life at work or at home means aligning all those areas of your life that will satisfy the drivers that dominate your present activities and your future dreams. You may even wind up making dramatic changes in one or the other or in both.

You may want to change your life goals, or you may want to change those things you're doing that will not meet those needs, wishes, or desires. Another way of saying that is, you may want to change your priorities.

For the majority of people, the most severe problem they experience with this is the fear of making the changes at all. The fear usually comes from not knowing what to expect from things they do. Self-management planning helps reduce that ignorance and fear.

Chapter 7

The Action Plan—Making Things Happen in Your Life

You achieve goals, you reach milestones only when you do things to make them happen. To give what you do on the job or in the home direction and accuracy, you have to plan your activities as means for reaching your milestones, for achieving your objectives. The well-formulated goal statements give direction to your actions.

Spontaneity, creativity, innovation play important roles in being human. Spontaneity, however, often diverts us from our primary interests or requirements, and its payoff is often less valuable than controlled, goal-directed action. And creativity or innovation are almost always impossible without the discipline that liberates the mind to be creative or innovative—that is, to produce something unique and of value where nothing like it existed before or to recombine old ideas or elements into new and valuable designs.

A complete action plan consists of at least one goal, plus a set of objectives necessary for accomplishing that goal, plus a list of activities necessary for reaching the objectives. A well-formulated goal statement by itself merely keeps your mind on the outcome you want and the stages you think you'll have to pass through in order to get there. It explains why you're going to do something, but not what you'll do or how you'll do it. Here's where the questions that start with *what, who, when, where, why,* and *how* become important.

The accompanying worksheet shows how to take the Milestone's sub-section of a goal statement's Conditions Section and turn that list into a set of objectives from which the action plan is designed. You'll probably notice immediately that it looks very much like the Worksheet for Creating a Well-Formulated Goal Statement. Still, there are differences.

Activities—Planning Who, What, When, Where, and How

The first difference is that opposite the heading Target, I've inserted something that I earlier called a milestone—"My CPA earned." The Milestones section is also called Activities. The implications should be quite clear.

Each milestone is itself a minigoal, right? Therefore, each milestone can be stated as a well-formulated goal statement, with the milestone converted into a target, the deadline evaluated to be appropriate for this stage in the process, and the activities appropriate for reaching the objective listed.

It's proper here to say a word about why you should use the past tense for stating your objective's target. The past tense is used in order to help you focus on

Worksheet for Creating a Basic Action Plan

Target:	My CPA earned
Deadline:	By the end of next year

Conditions

Activities: *(to include what, who, when, where, and how)*

Register in the local college for the preparatory classes

Attend the classes and do all the assignments, passing all the courses with no less than a grade of B

Budget effectively to guarantee having money for tuition and books

Divide the chores between the children and myself in order to give myself time to study

Contingencies: Car breaks down, and I can't put away the money I need

The children don't cooperate

what you have to do to be successful at reaching your target. It's as if you're saying, "O.K., I've earned my CPA. Now, how did I do that?" You're *recalling* events as if they've happened in order to ensure that you include everything you need to do.

In this example, I've listed just a few activities only to illustrate what you should do next with your own planning. Use a separate page for each objective (milestone).

A blank copy of the form, which you can reproduce, is included in the Sample Forms section at the end of the book. When you've completed that part of the exercise, return to your reading on this page.

Contingency Planning—Playing "What If"

Here's where the winners get separated from the Alices of this world.

Very frequently, "Alice" (male or female) and many otherwise good planners fail to play "What if." It's a simple game, with easy-to-follow rules. Just think of all the possible things that could go wrong, all the pitfalls, all the obstacles that could get in the way of your reaching your target. Then, think of what alternatives you have for getting around them, or what steps you'll have to take to correct a problem or to eliminate a barrier. That's it. That's all there is to it (well, maybe not quite *all* there is to it).

Creating Your Own Action Plan

By listing all the activities and contingencies you can think of, you can develop comprehensive plans for achieving all your goals. You can even draw charts that will help you keep track of the more complicated plans.

What you see in the accompanying diagram is a modified version of what planning experts call a PERT chart (an acronym that stands for "Performance Evaluation and Review Technique").

The final goal is shown as a rectangle at the right end of the chart. Each milestone is shown as an oval in the pattern. And each activity or contingency is shown as a straight line between the milestones.

As you can see, the diagram resembles a road map, with several alternative ways to get to the same point. The only difference between a road map and this approach to planning is that in our chart, *the two paths may have to be followed in order to get to the one destination.* For example, if the goal in this situation is "car readied for the trip," one path might represent the process of renting the car (pricing, evaluating, and so on) while the other path represents the buying and packing of provisions—both of which activities could go on at the same time. If you add together the amount of time each activity should take, you'll be able to total the entire time each path could take. You'll also be able to

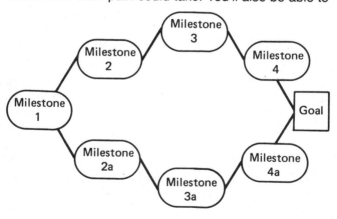

decide when you can start and complete each activity in the path.

So for the last part of your exercise, if you'd like to try it, take a Worksheet for Creating a Basic Action Plan that you've completed. Add some contingencies that could prevent you from reaching that milestone, plus some action steps for dealing with those contingencies, and draw a chart similar to the PERT chart shown earlier. Then, you're ready to take your first action steps.

After you do that last part of the exercise, turn back to read the final section of this book.

Chapter 8

Self-Management—
Now You Are in Control!

Now comes the time to put all that I've discussed into action. *The only way for Alice to have gotten Francine's job was for her to have put into action what I've preached.* If she had ever evaluated how she approached the world in which she lives and works, she would then have had some control over that world. That control would have been noticed by the people whose decisions sealed her fate. But it all begins with what she does to bring order and organization into that world.

That goes for anyone who wants to meet the needs, wishes, and desires that dwell within him or her.

All of that planning leads to order and organization only if it's applied to the realities of everyday activities. Goals and objectives direct your daily activities when you answer the questions What goals am I trying to achieve at this time? and Which are most important and should have my attention now? The answers to those questions then lead to, Toward what objectives do I have to work *today* in order to reach that goal?

From that point on, you know what you have to do today. *You have to do those things that will help you reach those objectives by the end of the day.* Your daily "to do" list now has three things Alice's workday lacked: focus, direction, and completeness.

How Alice Could Have Reached Her Target Through Self-Management

Let's take a look backward to see how careful self-management could have helped Alice get that quarterly expense report to Francine on time.

Alice's goal is to get Francine's job someday, right? Well, one objective Alice could have listed as a way to get that job is: Every day, demonstrate that I am efficient and can get my work done in a timely manner. That objective can be referred to with the shorthand phrase "Complete assignments."

October 1. Alice has an assignment: get her quarterly expense report to Francine by 9:00. In the sidebar on page 48, you can see how that appears on a format you can use to organize your own daily activities.

Right at the top of the page, you see the goal that dominates everything that Alice does. Every day, on a fresh page, she writes in the same goal until such time as she reaches it.

Daily Planner

Goal: To be manager of finance and accounting

Objectives to Achieve Today: 10/1/86	*Priority*	*Deadline*	*Status*
Quarterly expense report delivered to			
Francine	1	9:00	X
Shipping's payroll ledger corrected	1	Noon	X
Coaching session with Gloria			
completed	1	5:00	X

Things to Do	*Pri-ority*	*Dead-line*	*Status*	*Appointments*
Review report for	1	8:00		8:00
accuracy			X	8:30
Make 8 copies, collated	3	8:45	X	9:00 Francine/her off.
Make corrections	2	8:30	X	9:30
Deliver report to Fran-				
cine	4	9:00	X	10:00 Gloria/my off.
Meet with Gloria to	1	10:00		10:30
review shipping's				11:00
payroll ledger			X	11:30
Locate errors	2	10:30	X	12:00 Lunch with Al
Correct errors	3	4:00	X	1:00
Meet with Gloria for	1	4:00	X	1:30
coaching session	1	4:00	X	2:00
Review corrections,	2	5:00		2:30
identify problems,				3:00
and take corrective			X	3:30
action				4:00 Gloria/my off.
				4:30

48

On the next line she identifies the objectives to achieve that day that contribute to becoming manager of the department. She recognizes their priorities and their status. That X-mark gets entered at the end of the day or at the time the objective is reached.

Each activity, you'll notice in the sample, has a priority and a deadline, just as goals and objectives do. The same criteria apply to identifying realistic deadlines here as we've used for identifying realistic targets. They have to be within your reach.

The principles of importance, immediacy, and dependency apply here also. Indeed, I think the principle of dependency has a greater role to play here than it does elsewhere because *nothing happens if things that have to be done don't get done.*

A numbering system is used here to lay out your priorities. Use the number *one* for the highest-priority item or the action that has to be done first in order to do other things; use the number *two* to denote the items of lesser importance or those that depend on a No. 1 priority; and so on.

You probably also noticed that the listed activities have to be related to an objective above but that they don't have to be shown in chronological order at first, as with making corrections in and collating the quarterly expense report. The idea is to get on paper your entire list of things to do to achieve your goals and then analyze what's what. The priority ratings and the deadlines take care of any disorganization in your initial thinking. Few people ever think in a perfectly linear fashion, and that's O.K.

The way to adjust for activities not related to an objective is not to list them in Things To Do at all but identify them instead as appointments in the Appointments column, the way Francine's lunch date with her friend Al was handled.

If a particular activity is extremely important (say, calling the bank sometime today to get your balance), and setting a specific time for doing it doesn't work well, then you could list it in the To Do column but mark the priority space with an asterisk. That way you know you should do it but that it doesn't fit with your objectives at the top of the page.

Each time you complete an activity, mark it off with an *X*. That gives you a sense of accomplishment at various times in the day.

If you don't complete some activity, mark it with an *I*, for incomplete. That way you will be sure to carry over that activity and its correlated objective to the next day or to another day soon.

Sample Forms

Blank forms bring this book to an end: a blank you can use for setting up additional well-formulated goal statements, a form for setting up a basic action plan based on those goal statements, a form for developing your daily planning.

Evaluate your goals and the goals of the associations you have. Evaluate your objectives in terms of how well they fit with your goals, and evaluate what you're doing in terms of how well those activities help you reach your objectives. Then apply the entire system to your daily activities.

Getting control is up to you. After all, it's your life.

Worksheet for Creating a Well-Formulated
Goal Statement

Target: _____

_____

Deadline: _____

_____

Conditions

Milestones: _____

_____

_____

_____

_____

_____

_____

_____

_____

_____

_____

_____

_____

Contingencies: _____

_____

_____

_____

_____

Worksheet for Creating a Basic Action Plan

Target: _____
Deadline: _____

Conditions

Activities: *(to include what, who, where, when, and how)*

_____
_____
_____
_____
_____
_____
_____
_____
_____
_____
_____
_____
_____
_____
_____
_____
_____
_____

Contingencies: _____
_____
_____
_____
_____

Daily Planner

Goal:

Objectives to Achieve Today:	Priority	Deadline	Status

Things to Do	Pri-ority	Dead-line	Status	Appointments
				8:00
				8:30
				9:00
				9:30
				10:00
				10:30
				11:00
				11:30
				12:00
				1:00
				1:30
				2:00
				2:30
				3:00
				3:30
				4:00
				4:30

Index